TARANGINI

5

Swami Chinmayananda
and
Swamini Saradapriyananda

CENTRAL CHINMAYA MISSION TRUST

Total no. of copies printed upto May 2007 - 30000 copies
Reprint December 2009 - November 2011 - 2000 copies
Revised Edition September 2013 - 3000 copies

Published by:
Chinmaya Prakashan
The Publications Division of
Central Chinmaya Mission Trust
Sandeepany Sadhanalaya
Saki Vihar Road, Mumbai 400072, India
Tel.: +91-22-2857 2367, 2857 5806   Fax: +91-22-2857 3065
Email: ccmtpublications@chinmayamission.com
Website: www.chinmayamission.com

Distribution Centre in USA:
Chinmaya Mission West
Publications Division
560 Bridgetown Pike, Langhorne, PA 19053, USA
Tel.: 1-888-CMW-READ, (215) 396-0390   Fax: (215) 396-9710
Email: publications@chinmayamission.org
Website: www.chinmayapublications.org

Design and Illustrations: Blue Fish

Printed by: Usha Multigraphs Pvt. Ltd., Mumbai-13, Tel.: 24925354

Price: ₹ 120/-

ISBN: 978-81-7597-542-2

CONTENTS

Listen!
Ye Children
of
Immortal Bliss!

Eat Dear Coat, Eat Dear Hat

Ishwar Chandra Vidyasagar was a great pioneer of education in Bengal and was very famous in the intellectual circles of Kolkata and other big cities. However, he remained very simple and ordinary in his habits and dress.

Once a very rich man gave a dinner in honour of Vidyasagar, to which the elite of Kolkata was invited. The host's palatial residence was decorated and illumined for the occasion. One by one the cars started arriving and the guests alighted at the portico. They were received by liveried servants and respectfully conducted within.

Ishwar Chandra Vidyasagar too, arrived for the party. He was dressed in his usual simple Bengali dhoti and loose shirt and wearing ordinary country shoes. In the onrush of cars and other vehicles and the well-dressed guests, nobody recognised this simple man in his simple clothes. The haughty servants at the main gate told him to go away. Vidyasagar silently walked back.

It was time for dinner. All the guests had arrived except the chief guest. The host and his wife became anxious. Vidyasagar was noted for his punctuality. Why was he late today?

Was he held up by some urgent work? Should they send someone

to fetch him? Troubled by such thoughts the host was pacing up and down near the main gate, when suddenly he noticed a car coming in. The car stopped at the porch and the chief guest, Vidyasagar alighted. He was wearing a stylish suit. The servants rushed forward to receive him. The host took him to the place of honour at the head of the table. Dinner was served. All the guests waited for the chief guest to start eating. But he asked for another chair instead. When it was brought, Vidyasagar got up from his chair and occupied the other one. Then one by one he removed his coat, his necktie and hat and placing them on the chair of honour, said aloud, "Eat dear coat, eat dear hat."

Everyone was perplexed. They stared at him, wondering whether he had suddenly taken leave of his senses. The host and hostess asked him the reason for his strange behaviour. "How can your coat and hat eat food?"

Vidyasagar smiled and said, "I do not know who was invited here today, me or my clothes. When I came earlier in my usual dhoti and kurta I was not allowed to come in, but when I came in the car

wearing all this paraphernalia, the servants rushed to welcome me and allowed me in. It is my clothes that were allowed in and not me. So I am asking the clothes to eat."

The embarassed hosts understood what had happened at the gate and were profuse in their apologies to Vidyasagar for the grave mistake.

Mrita Sanjeevani Vidya

From time immemorial the gods and asuras have been at war with each other. Numerous bitter wars broke out between them in which many warriors were killed on either side. However, the asuras had one advantage over the gods. Their Guru Shukracharya knew the Mrita Sanjeevani Vidya, the science of bringing dead people back to life. Whenever the asuras died in a war, their Guru would bring them back to life again and thus they flourished. The gods, on the other hand, did not know this science and their numbers slowly dwindled. Once the gods held a conference to discuss ways and means of acquiring knowledge of this science. At last they decided that Kacha, the son of their Guru, Brihaspati, should be sent to Shukracharya's ashrama to become his disciple and learn this science.

Kacha took leave of the gods and came to Shukracharya. Though he was the enemy's son, Shukracharya accepted him as his disciple because the shastras say that a teacher should never turn away a sincere student. Kacha stayed in the Guru's ashrama and served the teacher along with the asura boys. Shukracharya found Kacha intelligent and industrious, obedient and honest and loved him dearly. Shukracharya had a daughter called Devayani who loved Kacha for his good manners and pleasant nature.

The asura boys did not like Kacha. They hated him intensely and tried to harm him in many ways. But they dared not do anything openly as their Guru and his daughter always protected him. Several years passed and Kacha grew up to be a handsome youth. He became adept in several sciences. With the passage of time the jealousy of the asura students also increased.

One day when all of them had gone to the forest to bring fuel for the ashrama, the asura boys killed Kacha. They threw his body into a pit and returned to the ashrama. It began to grow dark and yet there was no sign of Kacha. Devayani grew anxious and went to her father. Shukracharya, with his divine insight, understood that Kacha had been killed by the asura students and that his dead body was lying at the bottom of a pit. He used the Mrita Sanjeevani Vidya and brought Kacha back to life. Kacha climbed out of the pit and returned home safely.

The asura boys' plan had been defeated. So they conspired to destroy Kacha in such a way that he could not be brought back to life by their Guru. When an opportunity arose they not only killed him, but cremated his body, collected the ashes and mixed them in the Guru's drinking water. Not knowing what the water contained, Shukracharya drank it. The asura boys rejoiced. As evening approached and it became dark, Devayani became apprehensive because Kacha had not returned. She went to her father and told him of her fears and misgivings. He closed his eyes and tried to see where Kacha was. But this time, he could not find him anywhere. Where could he have gone? Then he turned his gaze inwards, and to his horror he found the boy's ashes in his own stomach. He realised what the asura boys had been up to.

With the help of the Mrita Sanjeevani Vidya he brought Kacha back to life once again. But how was Kacha to come out of Shukracharya's stomach? The Guru thought very hard and at last decided that there was only one way out. He told Kacha, "Son, I shall now teach you the Mrita Sanjeevani Vidya. Learn it from where you are. When you have learnt it thoroughly, tear open my body and come out. Then make use of your knowledge and bring me back to life. Kacha was very happy, for it was to acquire this knowledge that he had remained a student in the ashrama for so long. Now his desire was about to be fulfilled.

Shukracharya taught the science to Kacha who learnt it quickly. Satisfied that Kacha had learnt it correctly, Shukracharya told him, "Son, now do as you have been instructed." Accordingly, Kacha rent open Shukracharya's body, and the Guru fell down dead. As soon as he emerged, Kacha revived him with the help of his new knowledge. When Shukracharya came back to life, Kacha prostrated before him in gratitude and sought his permission to return home. Shukracharya blessed him and gave him leave to go.

But as he was preparing to leave, Devayani came to him and said, "Why do you want to leave us and go away? Why you do not marry me and settle down here?"

But Kacha had not even thought of such an idea. He said, "Devayani, you are the daughter of my Guru and so are like my sister. How can I marry you? I must return to my people."

Devayani was angry at his refusal. She cursed him saying, "It seems that you befriended me only to learn this science from my father. This is nothing but sheer deceit. You have cheated me. So you will never be able to use this science when you need it."

Kacha smiled gently and said, "Sister, you are angry and that is why you curse me. So be it. The science may not work for me but others who learn it from me will be able to use it."

Saying this, Kacha went back to the devas. From then onwards, the devas were on par with the demons and could revive their numbers as quickly as their enemies.

Shreeshaila Shikhara

Shreeshaila is one of the twelve jyotirlinga temples dedicated to Lord Shiva. The Lord here is known as Mallikarjuna and his consort as Bhramaramba. On Shivaratri, devotees gather here in large numbers. After worshipping the Lord they return home the next day. The temple is in a valley. From a certain point on the way, the temple shikhara which is the pinnacle, can be seen. The shastras say that the vision of the shikhara itself destroys the wheel of birth and death. Thus it is sung:

"Shreeshaila shikharam drishtva punarjanma na vidyate!"

In the olden days the temple was surrounded by thick forests inhabited by ferocious animals and robbers. It was dangerous to go through this forest not only alone but also in groups. Even those who reached the temple safely fell victim to malaria. Yet thousands of devotees continued to gather there for Mahashivaratri.

One year, as Shivaratri approached, Bhramaramba became pensive. She approached Lord Mallikarjuna and said, "Lord, every year so many devotees come for your darshana; so many of them will be liberated from the wheel of birth and death and will come straight to Kailash."

The Lord smiled and said, "Devi, people usually call me Bholanath. But you are even more gullible than I. Do you believe that they will all come to Kailash? Not even one of them may come here. They visit the temple but they have no faith. Only the truly faithful will be benefitted. So do not be nervous."

Bhramaramba was surprised and said, "How is that possible? So many people visit us. You mean to say that none of them is endowed with faith? Are you not underestimating their devotion?"

The Lord smiled enigmatically and said, "Let us see this Shivaratri."

Shivaratri came and there was a great throng of devotees at the temple. The Lord and Amba sat disguised as an old couple near the temple gate. The Lord lay as a very sick man about to die and Amba sat near him as his old wife. She had a sad face and every now and then she wiped the tears from her eyes. Near her was a small copper pot full of water with a copper spoon in it.

As the devotees neared the gate, the old woman cried piteously, "O good sirs. Be compassionate. My old man is dying of an unknown disease."

Since the temple was at the Lord's door, people with an eye to earn merit asked, "What can we do for him, old woman?"

She wiped away her tears with the corner of her sari and said, "O, please pour a spoonful of this water into his mouth, O pure hearted ones. You are all pure after the darshana of the shikhara. So he will certainly recover."

But the people had no faith. Were they really pure? Did the darshana of the shikhara really absolve them of their sins? They thought, what if the old man were to die after we give him water? That will certainly be a sin. So they all shook their heads and walked on, while the old woman's wails followed them, "Have mercy! Have pity!"

As it was getting dark, a very sinful woman came out of the temple. She, too, heard the lament of the old woman. She bent down to pour the water in the old man's mouth. The others around were aghast at her daring. "You are the worst of sinners! You have lived a life of sin for the sake of money. How can you take up the spoon? Even we, who are more virtuous than you, are hesitant. You will incur a greater sin if the old man dies."

The woman, whose face shone with the glow of faith, replied, "Have you not heard the assurance of the shastras, that having seen the shikhara all sins are destroyed. I have not only seen the shikhara but even worshipped the Lord. Even if my sins have still not been washed away, it makes no difference to me. One sin more will not matter. If I can save the life of this old man, it will be my greatest merit. I will give him water." Thus she poured the water into the old man's mouth. Immediately, the old couple disappeared and in their place stood Bhramaramba and Mallikarjuna shining and glorious. They blessed the woman, because of the thousands of devotees, she was the only one with faith.

18

The Kindly King

Once Maharaja Ranjit Singh who was known as the Sher-E-Punjab, the Lion of Punjab, was strolling in the palace garden, accompanied by his ministers and several attendants. Suddenly, a stone flew through the air and struck his forehead. Blood gushed out from the wound. The ministers and the attendants were aghast. They ran out of the garden to find out who had thrown the stone. After some time they found the stone thrower and returned to the Maharaja with the culprit.

It was a poor old woman. She trembled with fear. The Maharaja looked at her and asked, "Woman, why did you throw the stone at me?"

Trembling with fear the old woman cried out, "O King, pardon me. I did not throw the stone at you. I did not imagine that you would be taking a stroll in these grounds. My son has not eaten for three days and is starving. I threw the stone at these mango trees which are full of ripe fruit. If I had been lucky, the stone would have hit the fruit and my son's hunger would have been satisfied. Unfortunately I hit you instead. Please pardon me Maharaja. Do not punish me. I did not intend to hurt you."

As he listened to the woman's words, tears welled up in Ranjit Singh's eyes. He turned to his ministers and said, "I never knew that there was

such poverty in my kingdom. Please send enough food for this woman's family immediately and also provide them with arable land so that they will have enough food in the future."

The ministers were surprised at this strange order. "Maharaja, this woman has injured you. Why are you being kind to her?"

The Maharaja smiled and said, "Had the woman succeeded in hitting the mango tree, her son's hunger would have been appeased. Instead she hit a Maharaja. Should she not get much more from me than she would from the tree? Her son's hunger must be removed forever."

The woman shed tears of joy and thanked the king. The ministers too, learnt a lesson from the Maharaja's generosity.

Fear of Death

A man was once crossing a river in a boat. As the water lapped the sides of the boat, it created a pleasant sensation. Feeling comfortably superior, he condescendingly asked the boatman.

"My good man, what was your father's occupation?"

"He was a boatman, Sir."

"And your grandfather?"

"He also ferried a boat, Sir."

"Are there many accidents on the river?"

"Sometimes there are Sir. My father died in such an accident and so did my grandfather."

The man looked at the boatman in wonder and asked, "My dear man, both your father and your grandfather died in boat accidents. Are you not afraid of ferrying a boat?"

The boatman smiled and asked, "Sir, where did your father die?"

"He died while asleep in bed," replied the man.

"And your grandfather?"

"He also died in bed," the man replied.

The boatman asked, "Sir, your father and grandfather both died while sleeping. Are you not afraid of sleeping in the bed?"

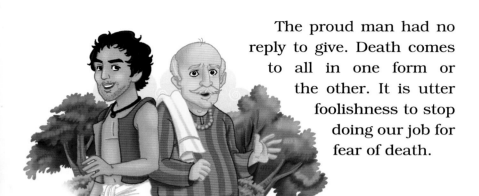

The proud man had no reply to give. Death comes to all in one form or the other. It is utter foolishness to stop doing our job for fear of death.

The Power of Satsang

Once, Narada went to Vaikuntha and asked Lord Narayana, "Please tell me, Bhagavan, what is the result of being in the company of good people?"

The Lord said, "Go to a certain forest on earth. There you will find a banyan tree, on the left branch of which is the nest of a parrot. In the nest will be a newly hatched baby parrot. Ask the baby bird what the result of satsang is. It will tell you."

Narada went to the tree post-haste. As he reached the nest, an egg hatched and a tiny parrot emerged. Narada approached the bird and asked, "Baby bird, please tell me what is the effect of satsang?" The moment the sentence was uttered, the baby bird fell down dead. Narada was shocked.

He went back to Narayana and told him that even before answering him, the bird had died.

Then Narayana told him to go to a certain village, where a new calf had taken birth in the house of a brahmin. "Question the calf and get the answer."

Narada went to the village and found the house of the brahmin. The calf was just getting up on its legs. He asked, "Dear calf, please tell me what is the result of satsang?"

Before he had finished speaking the calf fell down dead.

Narada was overpowered by guilt and sadness.

"What a sinful person I am!" he thought. "I appear to have been responsible for two deaths."

Grieving, he went to Vaikuntha and told Narayana what had happened. Narayana consoled him and said, "Do not worry, it is not your fault. Now a foal is being born in the king of Kashi's stable. Go and ask the baby horse." Narada went to the stable as directed and questioned the baby horse as soon as it was born. Here, too, the baby horse died as soon as the question was put to him. Narada was now in despair. He had three deaths on his conscience! What mistake had he made in

approaching these newborn babies? He had followed the Lord's directions in each case. Then how had such tragedies occurred?

Puzzled and confused he went to Narayana and reported the death of the foal. Looking at Narada's harrassed face, the Lord smiled and said, "Despite all your trouble, you have not got your answer. Now do one thing. A son has just been born to the king of Kashi. Go and ask the baby your question."

Narada's face grew pale with fear. "No more, Lord," he cried out. "I can not bear any more deaths on my conscience. Let my question remain unanswered. I am already weighed down with guilt. I can not have the death of a prince on my conscience as well."

Narayana smiled and assured him, "This time you will get the answer to your question"!

Thus assured, Narada went to the King of Kashi's palace. There was great rejoicing in the palace because of the birth of a prince. When the king saw Narada, he considered himself doubly blessed. He brought the young prince for the sage's blessings.

Narada picked the baby up and cradling it in his arms asked, "Baby, please tell me what is the result of satsang?"

The baby gurgled happily and said, "O sage, have you not understood yet? I was the baby bird whom you questioned. Because of the brief contact with a saint like you, I got released from that tiny body immediately and was born as the calf. There again you came and questioned me. By that short contact, I got rid of my insignificant birth and was born as a horse. Again you asked me the same question. By that contact, I am now born as the prince of Kashi. This is the result of satsang. I am grateful to you, O sage, for elevating me to this stage."

On hearing this, Narada finally understood the power of satsang. He was no longer sad or guilty at the deaths of the baby animals. He blessed the prince and, singing the Lord's glories, went his way.

Nectar From Heaven

Kashyapa Brahma had two wives, Vinata and Kadru. One evening, they went to the seashore for a stroll. There in the distance they saw Indra's beautiful white horse. They were both enchanted by its beauty and gazed at it with admiration.

Vinata said, "Look sister, how white the horse is. Rarely does one see such a pure white horse."

"Yes, yes," agreed Kadru. "But its tail has black bands. But for that, the horse would have been much more beautiful."

Vinata was surprised. She looked hard at the horse but could not find any black bands on its tail! She said, "Perhaps you cannot see properly. There is no blackness at all in the tail. Look at it again."

Kadru insisted that the tail was black. They got into an argument and finally they laid a bet. If the horse's tail was white, Kadru would serve Vinata as her slave; if the tail was black then Vinata would become Kadru's slave. Then Vinata said, "All right, let us go near the horse and check its tail."

"Not now," said Kadru, "it is already dark, we will examine it in the morning." Vinata agreed and they returned home. As soon as Kadru reached home, she called all her children together and told them about her bet with Vinata. Kadru was a serpent-maiden so her children were snakes. They were surprised when they heard about the bet. They said, "Mother, why did you lay such a bet at all? Indra's horse is pure white. Tomorrow morning when you discover this, you will have to serve Vinata as a slave for life. Why did you do such a foolish thing?"

Kadru smiled slyly and said, "Of course I know that the horse is pure white. But I wanted Vinata to be my slave. That is why I proposed such a bet. Now I want your help. You are black in colour. Tomorrow morning, before Vinata and I go to the seashore, you go there and wind yourselves round the tail of the horse so that it appears black."

Kadru's children were shocked at the proposed deception and refused to be a party to it. Kadru grew angry with them and threatened to curse them. So one of them, called Karkotaka, agreed to do his mother's bidding.

Early next morning Karkotaka reached the seashore and wound himself around the tail of the white horse. After some time, Vinata and Kadru came there. Now the horse's tail appeared to be black even from a distance. There was no need to go closer and confirm the colour. Vinata was dejected. But she had lost the bet. So she had to become Kadru's slave.

Many years passed. There was no help in sight except that Vinata was lucky and happy to have a powerful son Garuda. But as the son of a slave woman, he too had to serve his stepmother and stepbrothers. He was at their beck and call all the time. Garuda could not understand why he should serve his stepbrothers. So one day he enquired from his mother as to how she became Kadru's slave. On hearing the whole story, he wanted to be released from the bondage of slavery.

He approached his stepbrothers and asked them on what condition they would agree to release his mother and him. They replied that they would release Garuda and his mother from bondage if Garuda could bring them the pot of nectar from heaven.

Garuda flew straight to heaven with his parents' blessings. He entered the palace, where the pot containing the nectar was carefully guarded by the celestials. He fought and defeated the celestials who were keeping a watch over the palace, and flew away with the pot. The defeated celestials raised a big hue and cry and all the gods came rushing. When they found that the nectar had been taken away by a mere mortal, they grew angry and pursued him. Garuda fought all the gods with his powerful wings and continued his flight. The gods were unable to stop him. Indra, the king of gods, approached Garuda and enquired why he was stealing the nectar from the gods. Garuda then explained his own predicament to Indra. He had to steal the nectar, but he suggested to Indra that there might be a way out. He said, "O King of gods, my step-brothers are the source of all our miseries. I do not want them to enjoy the nectar, though I am carrying it for them. The moment I hand over this pot to my brothers, we will be free and I shall take my mother away from there. Could you not steal the nectar back? They will not be able to stop you."

Indra was pleased at this suggestion. He praised Garuda for his devotion to his mother and blessed him. Garuda flew to his brothers and called all of them together. He placed the pot of nectar on a seat made of darbha grass and said, "Look, here is the nectar from heaven.

Now, fulfill your promise and release my mother and me from slavery."

The brothers were happy beyond words when they saw the nectar. They proclaimed in one voice that now Garuda and his mother were free. Garuda asked his mother to climb on his back. As he made ready to fly away, he gave some parting advice to his brothers, "Brothers, you know that this is the sacred nectar from heaven. Before you drink it, take a bath and become pure, otherwise it will not be of any use to you." And flapping his wings he flew away with his mother.

The snakes rejoiced at their good fortune and, as suggested by Garuda, went to take a bath. Indra was hiding nearby and seeing this opportunity he immediately snatched up the pot. One of the brothers saw him and cried out, but by the time they all came running to protect the pot of nectar, it was too late. Indra was already far away. They gazed at his receding figure with rage and frustration until it disappeared from view. Looking at the empty seat

of grass they saw a few drops of nectar that had fallen from the pot. They eagerly crawled towards the seat and licked the drops of nectar. The sharp points of the grass tore their tongues. Since then all snakes have a forked tongue.

Shuka Yogi

Shuka was a great yogi. When he was still in his mother's womb, he knew the world would be full of distractions. So though the nine months of confinement were over he chose not to be born. One, two, then twelve years passed. Yet there was no sign of the child. His poor mother found it difficult to move about with a twelve year old boy in her womb, but she did not know what to do.

She appealed to her husband, Maharshi Vyasa. Vyasa requested the boy to come out quickly. But the boy replied that it was safer for him inside the womb. If he came out he would be exposed to the snares of the world.

Then all the gods appealed to Shuka. The boy gave them the same reply. But they persisted, "Your mother finds you too heavy to carry within her. You are a great yogi. How can the world drag you down with its fascinations? It can ensnare only small people. Please come out."

On these repeated requests Shuka came out, as a twelve year old youngster. All the gods gave him their blessings. Within a very short time he realised the highest Truth of his own accord.

But as he had no Guru, he thought perhaps there was something more to be learnt.

He went to his father and asked for his guidance. Maharshi Vyasa said, "Son, you have already reached the supreme Goal. Beyond that, there is nothing." But Shuka was not convinced. So Vyasa directed Shuka to Mithila to be instructed by King Janaka.

Shuka thought, 'Janaka is a householder and a king. How can he instruct me?' But he obeyed his father and went straight to Mithila.

At Mithila, he was not allowed inside the gates as he did not have the king's permission to enter. Shuka remained at the gates for seven days. No one paid any attention to him even though he was the son of the great Vedavyasa. But Shuka waited patiently.

On the eighth day the king came with a huge retinue and welcomed him with due reverence. He took him in a procession through the streets of Mithila to a palace which was meant for his stay. Hundreds of beautiful ladies were employed to serve him. Dainty dishes were prepared to satisfy his taste buds and he was treated to lavish hospitality. But all this pomp and show did not move Shuka in the least. For, in his mind was the one thought of being instructed in the science of the Reality.

One day, he was invited to attend the court. Here King Janaka and his courtiers were being entertained with dance and music. Shuka sat on the seat to which he was led, neither revelling in the entertainment nor showing any aversion to it.

Then King Janaka gave him a vessel brimming with oil and asked him to go round the hall seven times, taking care not to spill a single drop. Shuka took the vessel of oil in his hand. He looked neither left nor right but walked around the hall seven times. He was distracted neither by the entertainment nor by the rich decorations of the hall. When he had finished the rounds he gave the vessel back to Janaka. Not a drop had been spilled.

Then King Janaka asked Shuka to open his mouth and put a piece of sugar candy in it.

He told him to keep it there for fifteen minutes. At the end of fifteen minutes Janaka looked in his mouth. The sugar candy was as it was when it was put in his mouth. Not a bit of it had melted, nor was there a trace of saliva on the tongue.

Janaka was happy with the perfect example of Realisation in front of him! He told Shuka, "Son, you have nothing more to learn or achieve. You have reached the supreme Goal. Go back in peace."

Shuka prostrated to King Janaka and returned home.

The Merchants And The Thieves

Once ten merchants went to a neighbouring kingdom for business. All their merchandise was sold and they earned a good profit. They were very happy. With their purses full of money, they started their return journey. They had to pass through a lonely forest. When they were half way through, three robbers with deadly weapons blocked their path. They threatened to kill them if they did not give them all their money and valuables. They ordered the merchants to take off their rich clothes and wore those themselves. Then they discovered food packets and a few bottles of wine. Soon they were eating and drinking to their heart's content.

While they were making merry, the poor merchants huddled under a tree, wondering whether they would be left alive. One of the thieves looked at them and with his mouth full shouted, "What are you doing there? Come on, dance and sing and entertain us while we eat."

The other two laughed at his words. The merchants did not know any song or dance and looked at each other.

The thief got angry and shouted, "Will you dance or should I kill you?" So saying he drew his sword.

The frightened merchants pleaded for mercy, agreeing to dance. "Go on, go on," cried the thieves.

One of the merchants was shrewd and did some fast thinking. From the way the thieves talked and behaved he knew they were illiterate. The merchants were all educated, and also spoke English. So he thought of a plan to overpower the thieves and whispered to the others, "Pretend to dance and listen to what I say. We shall overpower them."

He stretched out his hands and started dancing. The others followed suit, carefully following what he was singing and repeating it so that the thieves would not suspect anything. The leader sang, while the others followed in chorus:

Ten, ten, ten, we are, ten we are.

Three, three, three they are, three alone;

We sing and dance, we laugh and clap

We sing and dance and laugh and clap

Singing, dancing, laughing, clapping

Round and round and round we turn.

We turn and twist, we twist and turn

Twist and turn and turn and twist

Then we part in three, groups of three

And three in a group

In three and three we turn and twist

In the centre stands the tenth.

We dance and clap, we laugh and clap

In groups of three we reach the thieves

Each three to catch one,

One thief for each group.

The tenth of us to bind them all.

As the leader sang the others understood his instructions. The thieves could not understand what they were singing. While the merchants danced and jumped in groups of three, the thieves roared with laughter. Suddenly the merchants moved close to them and caught them. The tenth merchant took a rope and tied them hand and foot. The merchants recovered their money and handed over the thieves to the police.

Parashurama

Parashurama was the sixth incarnation of Lord Vishnu. Every time dharma declines and adharma increases, the Lord incarnates on earth to vanquish the evil doers and protect the good people.

Parashurama was born to sage Jamadagni and his wife Renuka. Though a brahmin, he excelled in warfare and his special weapon was the parashu or axe. Once, when he was away from his ashrama, King Kartaveeryarjuna along with a huge retinue happened to be a guest there. Kartaveerya was a very powerful king. He had a thousand arms. At first he hesitated to stay in the ashrama because he thought it would be difficult for a sage dwelling in the forest to provide his retinue with food and other conveniences. But the sage assured him that there would be no difficulty.

His cow, Kamadhenu, would yield all that was needed to serve the king and his people. This was proved true. The divine cow provided sumptuous food, tents for them to stay in, cots and mattresses, and whatever else was needed.

The king was amazed at the power of the cow, and thought that it would be so nice to possess her. He asked Jamadagni to give the cow to him as she would be of great use in the royal palace. He was prepared to pay any price for her. But the sage refused to part with the cow saying that she was not for sale.

Kartaveerya was very disappointed. He was angry that the sage had dared to refuse his request. In his arrogance, he took the cow away by force.

There was nothing the sage and other ashramites could do to stop him.

When Parashurama returned to the ashrama, he learnt about Kartaveerya's high handed behaviour and the loss of the cow. He became very angry. Armed with his parashu, he went to the king's palace. With one blow of the axe he killed the king and brought back the cow. Neither the huge army nor his many sons could stop Parashurama. Smarting under their helplessness they swore to take revenge on Parashurama for killing Kartaveeryarjuna.

So they watched the ashrama closely and one day when Parashurama was away they invaded it. They caught sage Jamadagni, mercilessly killed him, and escaped before Parashurama returned. Poor Renuka, wept inconsolably by her husband's dead body. Parashurama heard his mother's cries and rushed back. He heard her call out twenty one times before he reached the ashrama. When he came and learnt what Kartaveerya's sons had done, his anger knew no bounds. He understood that this was not a stray case of one royal family injuring the innocent. The kshatriyas had become tyrants. It would only be a matter of time before things would get out of control.

He took up his parashu and went around the country killing all male members of the royal families including the children and old men. Since his mother had cried out to him twenty one times, he went around twenty one times to deal with the haughty and arrogant warriors. Dasharatha, the King of Ayodhya was the only one to escape because he hid in the apartments of his queens, dressed as a woman.

After his task was accomplished, Parashurama's anger subsided. To wash away the sins of this terrible bloodshed, he went on a pilgrimage and took a bath in the sacred Samantapanchaka Tirtha. Thus purified, he gave the territory he had won to Kashyapa rishi. As he had given everything away, he had no place to stay. So he went to the west coast of India and begged the ocean to give him some land. The ocean consented and withdrew a bit yielding some land from under its waters. The land thus given by the ocean is the present state of Kerala.

Doing God's Work

Chhatrapati Shivaji established the empire of righteousness and ruled the Maharashtra empire under the banner of the orange coloured flag as a representative of his Guru, Samartha Ramadasa. In all matters of administration of the empire, dharma was his guiding principle, and his Guru advised him on all vital matters.

Shivaji was righteousness personified and very powerful and intelligent. He defeated the Moghul army a number of times. He carved out his empire from the land thus won from the Muslim rulers. He had to be on the alert all the time because his enemies were looking for a chance to kill him. Though his life was in danger every minute, he would not stop his activities.

He came to hear of Sant Tukarama and his all night kirtanas which were elevating and exhilarating. He was very anxious to attend at least one such event and immerse himself in the divine singing, oblivious to everything else.

Unknown to anyone, one night he joined the kirtanas and sat in the front. Though he did not announce himself, Tukarama knew him through his divine vision, and prayed to the Lord that no harm would come to the Chhatrapati. Soon, the kirtana started and Tukarama stood up in ecstasy singing and dancing. The audience too stood up to accompany him. Shivaji was transported to another realm altogether. He hardly knew himself. When the kirtana was at its climax, and no one was conscious of anything except the Lord's name, the Muslims who were watching, thought now was the time to catch Shivaji and kill him. Disguised as Hindus, they entered the assembly and started searching for Shivaji in the huge crowd.

But, a miracle happened! Tukarama's prayer was answered. To the search party everyone that was gathered there looked like Shivaji. Who among them all was the real one? For hours they searched but in vain. Frustrated, they left the place.

When one is doing God's work, God protects him and no harm can come to him.

न हि कल्याणकृत्कश्चिद्दुर्गतिं तात गच्छति।।

na hi kalyaanakrtkasciddurgatim taata gacchati

(Bhagavad-gita Chapter 6-40)

Jarasandha

Brihadratha was the mighty king of Magadha whose wives were the twin daughters of the king of Kashi. When he married them, he took a vow not to show any partiality to either and to treat them on an absolutely equal basis. They lived happily together but when they remained childless even after a number of years, all three of them went to a forest and underwent severe tapas.

One day Sage Kaushika of the Gautama family noticed them and came to know about their desire. He felt sorry for them and wanted to help. At that time, a ripe mango fell into his lap. He picked it up and gave it to Brihadratha, saying that the mango would fulfil his desire.

The happy king divided the mango between his two wives. They ate the mango and in time, the two queens gave birth.

To their amazement, they both had only half a child, with half a head, one eye, one ear, one arm, one leg and half a torso. Neither baby was alive. Even if it had been, what was the use? How could such a baby be brought up?

The horrified nurses threw the two halves outside the palace gates. That very day a demoness called Jara was wandering in the streets of Magadha. She found the two pieces and put them together. When they were joined, the baby came alive and started to cry. The demoness was a friend of Brihadratha, and she knew these were the babies born to his queens. So she brought the baby, now whole, to the king who was overjoyed. He took the baby from Jara and carried him to the two queens who received him with tender love. Their sorrow changed into joy when they saw that the baby was well and normal. The two mothers brought him up with great love and care. Since he was joined together by Jara, he was called Jarasandha.

In time, Jarasandha grew up to be a powerful king, but he was demoniacal by nature. He imprisoned a thousand kings in order to sacrifice them so that he would become invincible. The whole of Aryavarta was shocked, but no one had the power to stop him.

When Dharmaraja Yudhishtara wished to perform the rajasuya yagna, he asked Krishna how successful it would be. Shri Krishna said that Jarasandha was the only king who might challenge Dharmaraja's supremacy and that if he was removed beforehand, the yagna could be performed successfully.

In order to accomplish this, Krishna, Bhima and Arjuna went to the kingdom of Magadha.

The king received them and asked what had brought them there. Krishna revealed their identities and said that they came as enemies and wanted to fight with him. Jarasandha would have to choose which one of them he wanted to fight.

Jarasandha sneeringly said, "Krishna, you are a cowherd. I cannot fight with you. Arjuna is too young and too frail. Bhima is my equal. I shall fight with him."

A day was fixed and many spectators gathered to watch the mortal combat. They chose to wrestle.

They wrestled for a long time neither gaining the upper hand. Suddenly, Bhima caught Jarasandha unawares and tore him into two pieces from head to foot. The two pieces fell down and Bhima heaved a sigh of relief, thinking that the fight was over. To everyone's surprise the two pieces swiftly moved towards one another and joined again into one whole. Jarasandha got up once more appearing refreshed and rejuvenated.

Poor Bhima was already exhausted, but his enemy was as fresh as ever, ready for another fight. He continued wrestling and once again tore Jarasandha into two pieces from head to foot. Incredibily the two pieces came together again and once more a refreshed Jarasandha was in the arena to resume the fight.

This happened two or three times. Bhima was thoroughly tired. How long could he continue? In desperation, he looked at Krishna, not knowing what to do. Krishna flashed him a smile of encouragement and made a sign, tearing a straw into two and throwing the pieces in opposite directions.

Bhima understood the hint. He fought with greater vigour and tore his opponent into two halves as before, but this time he carefully threw the pieces in opposite directions so that the two sides were not face to face. The two bits could not join as before and the terrible Jarasandha was finally defeated.

All the kings Jarasandha had imprisoned were set free. Sahadeva, the son of Jarasandha, was installed as king of Magadha. The three triumphant heroes returned to Indraprasthanagara, to report their victory to Dharmaraja, so that the yagna could now be performed.

The Unwanted Guest

Scene One

(As the curtain rises, Hema, a middle-class housewife is seen sweeping the floor, gathering the dirt, pieces of paper, cigarette stubs, etc. and throwing them into the wastepaper basket. Anil, her husband seated on a chair, looks on with disgust.)

Hema: *(rising to her feet)* There, at last. It's over. The room is clean again.

Anil: Useless fellows. It is a wonder how they can turn our beautiful room into a pigsty. Why can't they be a little cleaner in their habits? There is a wastepaper basket right here, but they must throw cigarette stubs on the floor in all directions. Ink spots everywhere! Chhi, chhi.

Hema: I don't know how they live in their own houses. Will their wives tolerate such behaviour? Every minute a new demand! A special dish every day! They must be eating like Maharajas to judge from their demands here.

Anil: Maharaja, my foot! I daresay they can't even afford a square meal in their own homes. That is why they are so greedy. I don't know whether you have noticed or not, ever since we came here two years ago, there has not been a single day when we have not had guests. The whole lot appears to think that we have a house here just for their convenience. Some work in the secretariat, and they drop in to stay with us; a medical check-up in the hospital and they come and lord it over us here! Its getting too much. This house is no better than a dharmashala.

Hema: *(sighing)* No picnics, no cinemas. It seems like ages since we went to a movie by ourselves.

Anil: All this is because our city is too near the village. Uncle's relatives, aunt's friends, brothers' classmates and their acquaintances! Oh God, why did you create a being called 'guest'? Had it not been for the 'guest', your world would have been a perfect place to live in. I admire you very much for all the wonderful things which you made for us, but why on earth did you make guests?

Hema: *(laughing)* No point asking why He made guests. There they are, in flesh and blood. Each one of them invading our house and destroying our peace. What do you propose to do about it?

Anil: I shall improve upon God's creation by ridding our house of all guests. The moment a guest comes I shall show him the door.

Hema: *(smiling)* Tall talk. You know you can't do it, I can't do it. The moment a guest comes, you will be all smiles to welcome him.

I shall be all smiles to serve him. Neither of us will be able to say what is in our minds.

Anil: Too true. That is our weakness. Somehow we must make a plan so that no guest remains with us longer than a week.

(The curtain falls.)

Scene Two

(The same scene two days later. Anil is sitting in the chair, tying his shoelaces. He finishes and stands up ready to leave for the office. As he moves towards the door, an old man enters with bag and baggage. Anil stares at him.)

Old man: Babu, you are Anil Kumar, aren't you? *(Anil nods his head)* Phew! Then I have come to the right place. Your uncle gave me perfect directions.

Anil: My uncle?

Old man: Yes, Rama Shastri. When I mentioned to him that I was going to the city on some work, he pressed me to come and stay with you. We have been great friends from childhood, you know. He would have felt bad had I not agreed to come here. What a great man your uncle is! So loving and affectionate.

Anil: *(smiling awkwardly)* Yes, yes, very affectionate. What is your name, sir, if I may ask?

Old man: I didn't tell you, did I? I am known as Ramanna. But your uncle calls me Ram.

Anil: Glad to meet you sir *(shakes hands with him, then looks at his wristwatch)* Please treat this as your home, sir. Now I must leave you. I am already late for work. We shall have a leisurely talk in the evening after I return. Hema!

(Hema comes out. Anil indicates Ramanna to her and motions to her to take the guest inside.)

(The curtain falls.)

Scene Three

(The same scene. Anil and Ramanna are sitting. Anil is reading a newspaper while Ramanna is singing Bhaja Govindam shlokas in a rough unmelodious voice. Now and then Anil frowns at the bad chanting. Hema brings steaming cups of coffee for both of them. Anil takes his and begins to sip it.)

Ramanna: *(looks at the cup and breaks into a loud laugh.)* My dear girl, I am a double quota man, I told you. This won't be enough for even one gulp. Give me a bigger tumbler please, there's a dear!

(Hema is about to refuse, but she changes her mind and goes in. She returns with coffee in the big tumbler, which Ramanna takes with a grunt of satisfaction.)

Ramanna: *(sipping the coffee and smacking his lips in satisfaction)* Wonderful! Wonderful! Ah, daughter, this is real coffee. My daughter-in-law is hopeless. It is amazing how she can ruin even the best coffee. She will never get this taste even if she tries for a hundred years. *(Anil looks at him now and then with distaste but the old man is indifferent to his glances.)*

(The curtain falls and rises again to reveal Anil and Ramanna seated at the table for lunch.)

Ramanna: *(smacking his lips in appreciation)* Very nice, very nice. Beta Anil, you are very lucky indeed to have such a wife. She is an expert cook. My poor son is cursed with that daughter-in-law of mine. Brahmaji must have specially created her for my boy. Believe it or not she can't even cook ordinary rice. *(Anil makes a sound with his tongue to indicate his sympathy but does not talk.)*

Ramanna: My wife used to be a good cook, despite her ill-health. My daughters also were well-trained by her. By God, the good lady would never allow them to sit idle even for a minute. They could cook exotic dishes when they were hardly fifteen! *(Anil nods his head now and then, hardly encouraging conversation. The old man heartily continues his monologue.)*

Ramanna: Hema beti, please bring that wonderful pickle. Without it I don't feel as if I have eaten anything. *(Hema serves the pickle. After a while she brings buttermilk to the table.)*

Ramanna: *(seeing the buttermilk)* Oh, daughter, I already told you. Get me curd. Buttermilk does not suit me. In my house there are three buffaloes and a cow. I always finish my meal with thick white curd, or else I don't relish my meal.

Anil: *(suppressing a smile)* Sir, you are not feeling well. You came here for a medical check-up. Curd is not good for your health.

Ramanna: Health be damned! I don't believe in the new fangled notions of careful dieting for keeping good health. When I eat, I eat with a bang. What is life if you can't eat what you want? *(Hema goes in and brings curds in a vessel. Greedily taking the vessel from her hand, he empties all the curd into his plate before Hema can prevent it. Anil looks at him in exasperation. But the old man talks on without noticing.)* Thank you beti, thank you. May the Lord bless you!

(The curtain falls and rises again. The same scene. Ramanna enters with a towel on his shoulder.

He comes near the side entrance and calls out Hema's name. Hema comes out.)

Ramanna: Daughter, after my bath I am going out to meet the chief minister on urgent work. All my dhotis are worn out. They don't look appropriate for the occasion. Can you lend me one of Anil's good dhotis? Preferably a new one.

Hema: I'm sorry, uncle, he will get angry with me if I lend you his clothes without his permission. He doesn't like other people wearing his clothes.

Ramanna: *(looking hurt)* What beti, after so many days you still consider me an outsider? I love you both as my own children. You see, the chief minister knows Anil's boss quite well. I wanted to put in a good word for Anil. That is why I wanted a good dhoti. It is not for my sake. *(He looks hopefully to see if Hema changes her mind and brings him the dhoti, but finding her adamant, heaves a sigh and goes in.)*

Hema: *(smiles contemptuously)* A good word indeed!

(The curtain falls.)

Scene Four

(The bedroom at night. Hema is preparing paan and Anil chews the leaves as she gives him some.)

Anil: *(stretching out his hand)* More supari please. *(Hema empties the supari tin into his hand.)* Already over? We got it only last week.

Hema: *(smiling)* You forget uncle. When he takes paan, it is hand-fulls of supari and bundles of leaves. No half measures with him!

Anil: God bless uncle! When is he leaving? Any idea?

Hema: As far as I can see he is in no hurry.

Anil: I think we should carry out our plan and send him away.

Hema: Yes, it is high time. Unless you do something about it soon, he will never go. Today he wanted to borrow your new dhoti. He said he was meeting the chief minister who is a friend of your boss and wanted to put in a good word for you.

Anil: A good word for me! *(laughing)* What impudence. We have to send him away somehow. How should we do it? I feel rather embarrassed.

Hema: True. I too find it difficult to refuse him point blank. He goes on asking for things like a child. Perhaps, if he does not get them for a day or two, he will be forced to leave.

Anil: *(feeling very happy)* That's it. You've got it! That is how we can get rid of him.

Hema: How?

Anil: By stopping his food. If he starves for one or two days, he will pack up and leave by himself.

Hema: How can we do that when we are eating? Even if we don't invite him he will pick up his plate and serve himself.

Anil: No, it is no use. We will have to trick him!

Hema: What kind of trick?

Anil: Tomorrow morning when you are in the kitchen, I shall come and pick a quarrel with you. You talk back to me rudely and we will get angry with each other. You shout, then I'll shout. Then I'll pretend to beat you. You weep loudly and call for help. That should send him packing. What do you say?

Hema: *(laughs)* It sounds fine. How did you get this idea? *(after thinking for a while)* If he leaves after that, well and good. If he doesn't, what then?

Anil: If he doesn't leave, you lock yourself in the bedroom and weep and I will leave for work cursing. That ought to frighten him. He cannot withstand the prospect of starvation.

Hema: No, he can't forego his lunch, come what may. It is amazing, what an appetite he has, considering his age. All right dear, let's do it. But please remember not to beat me too hard, or else I will really have to weep.

Anil: Serves you right! With your nice coffee and tasty dishes you feed him so fully and now he doesn't want to leave.

Hema: Right sir. Next time a guest comes, I will put salt in the coffee and serve it to him.

Anil: Yes, and give it in a big tumbler, full to the brim. *(Both of them laugh heartily.)*

(The curtain falls.)

Scene Five

(The kitchen early morning next day. Hema is busy making coffee. Anil peeps in.)

Anil: *(winks at her and speaks aloud)* Seven o' clock and my coffee not ready yet! You have become quite lazy nowadays.

Hema: *(looks at him with a smile and replies angrily)* Who is lazy? Me? Nice thing to say. Here I am slaving away for you since six o' clock. You get up now and accuse me of laziness.

Anil: *(smiles approval and retorts angrily)* Wretched woman, what is it to you, when I get up? The man of the house runs around the whole day sweating and toiling for you... if he sleeps a little longer than usual you grumble. Who are you to question me? I will get up when I please seven, eight or ten o'clock. What are you here for if you can't give me coffee when I need it? Who do you think you are... a Maharani or something?

Hema: *(beating her head with her hands)* Maharani? Maharani? How can I be a Maharani, tied down to you? Had I married the Rao Sahib's son when he proposed, I would have been a real Maharani, by now. I was a fool. Who else but a fool would have consented to marry you?

Anil: So now it has come to this! You are too fine for me. You repent having married me. Why then do you stay with me? Go away immediately, leave before I throw you out. *(rushes towards her in great anger, catches hold of her hair and pretends to beat her.)* Leave the house immediately! You will not stay here even a minute longer.

Hema: Oh, oh, oh, oh. Help, help me. Help, my husband has suddenly gone mad, he is killing me... help... help... help!

(As the quarrel develops Ramanna comes two or three times and peeps in anxiously. He hesitates to interfere and goes back. Anil and Hema see him but pretend not to have done so. The third time when Ramanna goes back, Anil goes near the door and peeps into the hall to see what Ramanna is doing. He comes back with a smile and whispers.)

Anil: *(in a low voice)* Weep once again, loudly. He is packing up. In a minute he will be gone. *(loudly)* Shut up, you woman. I will finish you today. My father warned me not to marry you. I should have listened to him. Now 1 am suffering. Stop shouting. I shall tear you to pieces.

Hema: *(weeping loudly)* You are possessed by a devil today. Leave me alone, you heartless man! I don't know how I have lived with you all these years. Send me back to my father's place. I will not live here a single day more.

(Anil goes to the door and carefully peeps out, turns back and laughs heartily.)

Anil: At last! He's gone for good. What a relief!

Hema: *(wiping her streaming eyes)* Really? Has he gone away?

Anil: Yes, with bag and baggage. He would have interfered had he dared but thought better of it and retreated. *(Laughing uproariously again)* I must have looked like a ruffian. Ah, what a relief, we are free, at last. All alone by ourselves. Let us celebrate this occasion.

(As they are talking, Ramanna returns from the back door and peeps in through the kitchen window with sly, cunning eyes to see whether the quarrel is genuine or not. He is visible to the audience and not to the couple. He nods his head in comprehension when he sees them talking in a friendly way.)

Hema: *(giving coffee to Anil, and taking a cup herself)* Yes, let's celebrate! Yesterday when we planned it, I never imagined that it would be so successful. You must congratulate me. See, how nicely I wept without really weeping!

Anil: *(smiling)* Ah, ah, you want to take all the credit! Look at me, how nicely I beat you without really beating you! *(they both laugh).*

Ramanna: *(suddenly coming into the kitchen and joining in the laughter)* Ha, ha, ha, look at me how nicely I went without really going! *(he sits down along with them as they both look at him in dismay.)*

Ramanna: Beti, I knew you were both making fun of me. How jovial you are! I love you both! Dear, now won't you get me coffee in the big tumbler please?

(As Hema, morosely turns to get a big tumbler for Ramanna, Anil comes to a firm decision. He suddenly gets up.)

Anil: *(in a firm decisive voice)* Hema, don't. It is not necessary. Uncle, get up. *(Hema looks at Anil hopefully and with admiration while Ramanna is alarmed.)*

Ramanna: What? What are you saying? Hema is giving me coffee.

Anil: *(with unbending firmness)* Uncle, if you want a big tumbler full of coffee, go to the hotel and order four cups of special extra strong coffee. Don't expect anything more from us. We wished to avoid unpleasantness by not telling you directly to leave our house and created the fictitious quarrel. But if you are so inconsiderate as to come back again after all this, I will have to be blunt and point you to the door. *(pointing with the hand)* Get up and get out of the door immediately or else I shall call the police.

(As Ramanna meekly gets up and goes out, the curtain falls.)

Verses to Learn

क्षारं जलं वारिमुचः पिबन्ति
तदेव मधुरं कृत्वा वमन्ति।
सन्तस्तथा दुर्जन दुर्वचांसि
पीत्वा च सूक्तानि समुद्गिरन्ति॥

A cloud makes salt water sweet
And returns it to earth as rain
A saint even if he receives bitterness from others
Gives them sweet blessings in return

पिबन्ति नद्यः स्वयमेव नाम्भः
स्वयं न खादन्ति फलानि वृक्षः।
नादन्ति सस्यानपि वारिवाहाः
परोपकाराय सतां विभूतयः॥

A river drinks not its own water
A tree eats not its own fruits
A cloud enjoys not the life-giving rain
A saint's blessing is for others
Never for himself

साहित्य संगीतकला विहीनः
साक्षात्पशुः पुच्छविषाणहीनः।
तृणं न खादन्नपि जीवमान
स्तद्भागध्येयं परमं पशूनाम्॥

He who has no appreciation for literature, music
or art
Is a very beast without tail and horns
True, he eats no grass for his living
Is it not the good fortune of animals?

येषां न विद्या न तपो न दानं
ज्ञानं न शीलं न गुणो न धर्मः।
ते मर्त्यलोके भुवि भारभूता
मनुष्यरूपेण मृगाश्चरन्ति॥

They who have no learning
Who are neither disciplined nor possess Knowledge
They who are neither polite nor charitable
or dutiful
They are only a burden on this earth
And roam as beasts in the guise of men.

Code of Conduct for the Chinmaya Mission Members

Chinmaya Mission members should:

- Try to live up to and fulfil the motto as well as the pledge of the Mission.

- Daily spare time for meditation and scriptural study.

- Once a week, on a convenient day offer prayers at a nearby temple with members of their family.

- Discover a life of harmony at home and on no account create any domestic unhappiness.

- Have satsang at home with the children and other family members. Reading of the Ramayana, Mahabharata and Bhagavat Mahapurana in a language familiar to the children would be an important part of the programme.

- Greet other Mission members with 'Hari Om'.

- Inculcate the practice of daily offering pranams to the elders in the house.

74

Chinmaya Mission Pledge

We stand as one family
bound to each other with love and respect.

We serve as an army
courageous and disciplined,
ever ready to fight against
all low tendencies and false values,
within and without us.

We live honestly
the noble life of sacrifice and service,
producing more than what we consume,
and giving more than what we take.

We seek the Lord's grace
to keep us on the path of virtue,
courage and wisdom.

May Thy grace and blessings
flow through us to the world around us.

We believe that the service of our country
is the service of the Lord of Lords,
and devotion to the people
is the devotion to the Supreme Self.

We know our responsibilities,
give us the ability and courage
to fulfil them.

Om Tat Sat